PORTRAIT OF A VILLAGE
CASTLE RISING

Portrait of a Village: Castle Rising

Colin S. Dence, OBE

PRIVATELY PUBLISHED
1980

Published by Colin S. Dence
Hall Place, Castle Rising, King's Lynn, Norfolk

ISBN 0 9507080 0 3

Printed in Great Britain by Daedalus Press
Wisbech, Cambridgeshire

CONTENTS

ILLUSTRATIONS

ACKNOWLEDGMENTS

My thanks are due to a number of people who have helped me in the research that I had to undertake in writing this book. To the County Record office at Norwich with their extensive records of the past history of the Rising Estate, to Mrs Henry Howard who has allowed me to examine her personal collection of family records, to the King's Lynn Library and the King's Lynn Museum who have been most helpful in showing me their records and their collections of etchings, drawings and photographs of the village. Not by any means the least is Mr Michael Begley, who has kindly read my manuscript and has made many helpful comments and a number of corrections.

The illustrations I have used come from some of the above, and also from the quite extensive collection at the Norwich Castle Museum, who have kindly allowed me to photograph many of them. This book cannot be a detailed historical study of the village, but is intended to supplement the several scholarly studies of the historical monuments, and to say something about the people who lived there during its not uneventful history.

The following accounts of the Castle and Village have been consulted.

Francis Blomefield, *An Essay towards a Topographical History of the County of Norfolk*, 1805

H. Harrod, 'Castle Rising' in *Norfolk Archaeology*, vol. iv, 1855

William Taylor, *The History and Antiquities of Castle Rising*, 1860

Edward Beloe, F.S.A., *The Barony, The Borough and the Franchise – a sketch*, 1894

H. L. Bradfer Lawrence, *Castle Rising, A short history of the Castle, Honor, Church, and Borough*, 1932

Professor R. Allen Brown, M.A., DPhil., F.S.A., *Castle Rising*, 1978

THE ORIGINAL VILLAGE

The early beginnings

If you were to walk along the footpath which leads from the old school house in Rising, eastwards towards the Mill, and if you were to brave the tall bracken and the brambles of Caste Rising wood – once known as Goos Moor – and if you knew just where to look, you would find an ancient barrow, tumulus or siege castle, nobody is quite sure which. If it was a burial mound it must have been that of a person of some importance. An earlier historian thought it might have been the tomb of Hsris or Hsrisi, a chieftain who may have founded the village, but later research into local place names indicates that this romantic idea must give way to the prosaic reality that it was the 'brushwood' village, for in our Scandinavian beginnings the first letter of a place name is said to indicate the nature of the place. Similarly it may be that Sandringham was not the home of the family of Saendring, but simply the sandy part of Dersingham!

It is no good starting the story of Rising at this point, because we do not know enough about it. It is no good starting with the Romans either, for all we know about their visits to the area is the finding of occasional coins, or the finding of some Romano-British pottery. The Romans must have known the area, for their main route to their Brancaster fortress – Peddars Way – ran only a few miles to the east, but we do not know if there was a village at Rising then.

The first evidence of the existence of the village is the Domesday record, and for this we owe a debt to William the Conqueror, whose enlightened decision it was to order the writing of a record which was a catalogue of the people and their possessions. Risinga, as the village was called in Domesday, was an outlying estate of the manor of Snettisham of which it was a part. Here is what it says:

> 'Three ploughlands; then as now 12 Villeins, 38 Bordars, then 4 serfs now 3, and 14 acres of meadow; then as now 2 plough on the demesne, and 2 ploughs belonging to the men, and 7 sokemen [with] 24 acres of land, then as now 1 plough and 3 mills, and 12 saltpans and one fishery, and 3 sokemen [with] 60 acres of land; then as now 1 plough, 1 sokeman [with] 60 acres and 1 plough, and 28 Bordars and 1 plough and 8 acres of meadow and one mill and one saltpan.'

This needs a little interpretation. The expression 'then as now' referred to the dates of the King's accession in 1066, and the date of the survey 1086, and the Snettisham Manor was owned by Stigand who was Archbishop of Canterbury in 1070. Villeins and Bordars were tenants who owed their landlords all the year round agricultural service. Villeins were ranked above Bordars, and the latter rendered menial service for a cottage at the will of their lord. The sokemen were freemen who owed their landlords service of a lighter or honourable kind, such as the obligation to attend the lord's court and the performance of occasional services. The serfs were of course the lowest ranking of all and had few if any privileges, but it is interesting to note that the village had only three serfs out of a total of sixty-four heads of household.

The sixty-four Villeins, Bordars, Sokemen and Serfs used between them seven ploughs and had 166 acres of land under cultivation. No mention was made of animals, but as there were seven ploughs and usually eight horses were allowed for each plough, quite a number would have been kept. A demesne was a farm kept by the landlord for his own use.

The most important subsidiary industry was salt making, and Domesday records thirteen saltpans, all of which would have been about the high water mark and grouped around the estuary of the Babingley river which until about 1690 was tidal. Some of these salt pans can still be seen as depressions in the ground. Salt produced in this way was obtained by concentrating the sea water by heating it, and then removing the magnesium salts which were the first to separate out from the solution. As the evaporation continued, the pure sodium salt began to separate out and was collected and dried.

Another industry of some importance to the village was the mills, which used the water power of the Babingley stream either for grinding of corn, the making of paper or the fulling of cloth. The remains of only two of the mills are visible today. It would again have been the Babingley river that was responsible for the fishery that was recorded.

Domesday only recorded the heads of a household, and scholars usually take an average of five persons in each household, so that the sixty-four heads represented some 320 people. As the population of the village at the time of the last census in 1971 was 157, it can be seen that the village had about twice as many people then as it does now.

It was only shortly after the Domesday survey that Bishop Stigand was replaced by Odo, Bishop of Bayeux in Normandy, and his ownership ceased when he rebelled against the King and the Norfolk estates were granted to a Norman knight William d'Albini I, and our story only really gets under way when his son d'Albini II chose Rising as the site of his West Norfolk Castle and home.

It is easier to understand the history of the village if one realises that since Norman times it has had three distinct periods of ownership. The first period of about two hundred years was that of the Norman lords, for the d'Albinis rose in the King's service and received high honours from him. The second period, also of about two hundred years was the period of Royal ownership which started in 1329, when the last of the Norman lords died without issue, and Queen Isabella came to live in Rising. This period lasted until the time of Henry VIII, who gave the village and its estates to the Dukes of Norfolk, with whose descendants it remains until the present day.

In 1693 the estate was sold to another of the numerous branches of the Howard family, in order to recoup the losses forced upon the Duke's estate by the execution of no less than two of the Dukes of Norfolk, one in the time of Henry VIII and the other in the time of Elizabeth I.

At the beginning of the eighteenth century the records of the village become much more extensive mainly because of the fortunate survival of many of the letters of the agents to the estate written to the Lord of the manor who lived at Ashstead in Surrey. It is interesting that if the Lord of the Manor had lived in Norfolk we might not have had such extensive records on which we could draw for our information. The Howards were consulted by the agents about many of the day to day details concerning the running of the estate, and their letters throw a great deal of light upon the lives of the inhabitants. The agents were important people in the life of the village, they did not seem to have lived in the village, but in Wisbech or Lynn. One of them, James Bellamy, is commemorated by a marble tablet in the church.

The Norman Lords

Although, as every child knows, the battle of Hastings was fought in 1066, the colonisation of Britain by its new Norman masters was necessarily a gradual affair. The first Norman owner of Rising was Bishop Odo of Bayeux, but he was deprived of his estates when he favoured the cause of Robert Duke of Normandy, William the Conqueror's eldest son, who claimed the throne of England by hereditary right, in opposition to William Rufus the reigning monarch. The Norman soldier who was given the manor of Rising Chase was a knight named d'Albini, who had backed King Rufus's winning side. His estates spread over a large part of Norfolk and indeed of other counties, but he did not choose to live at Rising, but at the village of Buckenham a few miles south of Norwich. He founded the Abbey at Wymondham where he and his wife lie buried.

In Victorian days in excavations at the Abbey a vault containing two lead coffins was discovered near the site of the original high altar. In one of the coffins was the body of a woman embalmed and in a remarkable state of preservation, in the other, and very much smaller, contained the body of a prematurely born child. It is thought that these are the remains of Maud, wife of the founder of the Abbey, who died in childbirth. The founder was succeeded by William d'Albini II, with whom we are particularly concerned. He decided to build two castle homes, one a mile or two away from the older castle at Old Buckenham, and the other our own castle at Rising.

D'Albini II was by all accounts quite a character. Nicknamed 'The Strong' and a man of great courage, he fought at Tinchbrai in France in 1106. It is said that the victor in that battle was promised in marriage to the widowed Queen of France, but William had already promised to marry the widowed Queen of England, and therefore refused the French offer. Being naturally jealous, it is said that she enticed him to an interview in her garden where she kept a pet lion. When William refused to marry her, she had him cast to the lion but, not dismayed, he rolled his cloak round his arm, thrust it into the lion's mouth, and killed it by tearing out its tongue, which he sent to the Queen! He returned to England and married King Henry I's widow, Adeliza, and was granted in his coat of arms the figure of a tongueless lion!

William got more than a coat of arms, for as part of her dowry he obtained the castle of Arundel and became Earl of Arundel, Sussex and Chichester. Such were the rewards of marrying a widowed Queen! There were no less than six d'Albinis in all, the fourth being a witness at the signing of Magna Carta at Runnymede, and the last of the line died in 1243 when the vast estates were divided up by the four sisters of the last d'Albini – Maud, Isabel, Nicola and Cicely. The Castle Rising estates fell to the share of Cecily, who was married to a certain Roger de Montalt of Flintshire who had castles at Montalt in Wales, Neston and Hawarden in Cheshire, and many other estates.

Four descendants of Roger Montalt succeeded him, the last being Roger de Montalt who died in 1329. He is chiefly celebrated for having a quarrel with the mayor and burgesses of Lynn, who raided his house in the town, seized him and, under duress, made him promise to surrender his rights of collecting the fourth part of the profits of the Talbothe of Lynn, which was responsible for regulating the trade of the town. Robert took a suit against the people responsible, and was awarded the huge sum of £4,000 which was paid in instalments. Some of the documents in the case are preserved in the King's Lynn records, together with impressions of the handsome Montalt seal.

With the death of the last Montalt (incidentally spelt Monte Alto in some documents), his widow Emma de Montalt agreed to surrender all her rights and estates to the crown in return for an annuity of £400 paid by Edward III. She lived at Rising for two years after the death of her husband, and died in 1331 and was buried at Stradsett near Downham Market, where her grave may still be seen under the carpet of the main aisle of the church. So ended the rule of the estates by the Norman lords, and so began the royal occupancy of the castle by Queen Isabella of England.

The Royal Rulers

This period was very different from the last one, for no longer was there a need for a fortified residence in West Norfolk capable of resisting hostile attack. Rising therefore became a royal residence with the royal apartments outside the gloomy keep with its old fashioned domestic and sanitary arrangements. The foundations of the royal apartments, in the vicinity of the keep but within the ramparts, have recently been excavated by archaeologists of the Department of the Environment.

Queen Isabella was the widow of Edward II the weak king who thought more of the company of attractive young men like Piers Gaveston than he did of his powerful barons. With Roger Mortimer, who was said to have been her lover, she conspired against her husband, captured and imprisoned him, and did him to death in Berkeley Castle.

During the minority of Edward III, Isabella and Mortimer ruled the country until some of the barons seized power, proclaimed young Edward King, hung Mortimer and sent Isabella to luxurious life imprisonment at Rising! There is dispute about the degree of freedom she was allowed, but no one who has examined the records has any doubt that she was virtually free. There are records of her stay in Rising. Transactions that she had with the mayor and burgesses of that town included payments and charges in respect of presents sent to her by the King in London. At least one of the presents was a barrel of oysters of which no doubt his mother was very fond. There is no evidence that she was ever a prisoner in the castle.

There is a great deal of uncertainty about the character of Isabella. She was a Frenchwoman, the daughter of the King of France, but she was known also as 'the she-wolf of France', and she married Edward II who clearly was a weak king. Was she implicated in the murder of her husband in Berkeley Castle? We do not know for certain, although she was certainly living with Mortimer who must have been implicated in her husband's death. Her imprisonment was considered luxurious because her son gave her a pension of £3,000 a year, later raised to £4,000, no mean sum in those days. But doubts about the reality of her imprisonment arose because the king visited her more or less annually at Rising, and she travelled around her estates in Yorkshire, and to Hertford Castle, at which place she died.

This was hardly the life of a prisoner, for she was clearly much loved by her son, who in 1330 directed that a group of gentlemen should escort the Queen – 'my dearest mother' (*Materna Carissima*) – to Windsor for Christmas. In 1344 she was with the King and Queen at festivities at Norwich, and at least once visited Walsingham on a pilgrimage. She died in 1356 and was buried at the church of the Greyfriars in Newgate in the city of London. It is said that the heart of her murdered husband was buried with her. Alas the church and the adjoining monastery was demolished in the time of Henry VIII, and no trace remains of her tomb.

Castle Rising remained in royal hands for a further 186 years after the death of Isabella, but sadly the castle itself was in decline, as is noted in the record of several inspections of the estate, of which of course the castle itself was only a small part. Nevertheless it is remarkable that the keep has remained much as it was, when many other castles of the same age have disappeared entirely. It is probable that it must have been used and therefore maintained to some extent throughout the years. There is little more known of the royal period which is of interest, other than the way in which its royal masters clearly disregarded the wishes of Edward III as they were laid down in royal charters, which have fortunately survived. The story is worth telling.

Edward III conveyed the estate to Edward the Black Prince, Duke of Cornwall, and laid down that no one, not even the King himself, had the right to alienate it. Alas for the promises of kings – Richard II twice did so, first giving it to John Duke of Brittany, and when the latter died, to one of his uncles the Duke of Norfolk. The matter is of interest because Prince Hal, later Henry V, challenged the Duke of York's right to the estate of Rising in the courts, citing the Edward III charter, and the alienation of Richard II was reversed, and the succession to the estate was confirmed as going to the eldest son of the sovereign.

In spite of this, Henry VIII gave the estate away during his reign, once again to the Duke of Norfolk, so that for the second time the Howard family obtained the estate, and this time for good, for it remains with the Howards to this day. Professor Allen Brown points out that Henry VIII's action was just as illegal as that of his ancestor Richard II, and that by rights the Castle Rising estate belongs to Charles Duke of Cornwall – the Prince of Wales! It does seem rather unlikely that he would wish to challenge the Howard ownership, and take possession of his castle, even though he should have no difficulty in establishing his case. So ends the second and royal period of the estate's ownership.

The Howards

The Rising Estate actually returned to the Howards by means of an exchange, the Duke of Norfolk and his son the Earl of Arundel giving to the King certain manors near Ipswich in Suffolk in exchange for certain other manors in central Norfolk and Suffolk including that of Castle Rising and Gaywood.

Thomas Howard, Duke of Norfolk held the estate until his death, but his son did not possess them because Henry VIII trumped up charges against him, and he was thrown into the Tower and later executed on Tower Hill. It is hard to believe it in these days, but the main charge against him was

> 'That on several occasions he had been guilty of high treason, in that he concealed from the King that his son the Earl of Surrey bore the arms of St Edward the Confessor, which did only belong to the King. . . .'

His death was generally condemned as an act of great injustice by the King, but the latter continued his vendetta against the Howard family, and the new Duke was committed to the Tower, and only escaped with his life because the King died in the night before his execution. The Duke was freed in 1553 and his possessions restored, but the next Duke, Thomas, again fell into disgrace and was tried by his peers on a charge that

> 'in the eleventh year of the Queen's reign he had traitorously consulted to deprive her of her crown and life and seize the throne by the aid of foreigners, that unknown to the Queen, he had treated of marriage with the Queen of Scots.'

He too fell on Tower Hill. His speech on being found guilty is worth quoting

> 'This is the judgement of a traitor, and I shall die as true a man to the Queen as any liveth'. Knocking himself hard upon the breast he said 'I will not desire any of you to make petition for my life; I will not desire to live, I am at a point, and my Lords, seeing you have put me out of your company, I trust soon to be

in better company. Only I beseech you my lords, to be humble suitors to the Queen's majesty for my poor orphan children – God doth know how true a heart I bear to her Majesty, and how true a heart to my country, – Farewell my lords.'

So once again Castle Rising returned to the Crown, by confiscation, and the Queen granted the estate to the Earl of Oxford for a short time, until, the grant being revoked, it was given to Henry Howard, Earl of Northampton, who was the brother of the executed Duke Thomas. He lived until 1616, and died without issue. It was he who built the Trinity Almshouse, of which more later.

The estate then returned to Thomas Howard, Earl of Arundel, who was the grandson of Duke Thomas. In this family it remained until it was bought by a certain Thomas Howard of Ashtead, Surrey, who was the sixth son of the Earl of Berkshire and a member of another branch of the Howard family, with whose descendants it remains to the present day. These genealogical details are inevitable with a family as widely spread as that of the Howards, for they possessed many titles, several of which from time to time were possessed by the Lords of the Manor of Rising.

THE BUILDINGS

The Castle

There is very little in the records about the castle in the period which followed the death of Queen Isabella, except references in documents about the estate that the castle was now in decay. This is not surprising because there was no longer any defensive purpose for a castle on this site, and it was already two hundred and twenty years old at the time of Isabella's death, and was not unnaturally showing signs of its age. The date of the building of the castle is, by the way, accepted as being circa 1158, and this is arrived at by Professor Allen Brown from the legal documents recording the gift of the Old Buckenham Castle to the Augustinians, when d'Albini II started building his two new castles, one at New Buckenham, and the other at Castle Rising.

The earliest picture we have of the castle is the engraving by Buck of 1738, which shows ships in full sail on the sea in the background, and seems to take serious liberties with the local geography! It shows a few remains of the red brick curtain wall which used to surmount the ramparts, together with a large chunk of what must have been one of the defensive towers, of which there were three originally. These can be seen drawn in characteristic three-dimensional form in the map of 1588, of which I shall be talking later. This is only a tracing of the original, but it is charming and includes the whole of the Chase of Rising up to and including the town of Lynn itself, and right across to Sandringham in the north, showing Sandringham Lodge, an early predecessor of the present Queen's house. It also shows that our own castle was surrounded by an extensive park to the south and east. The drawing of the Castle by Millicent is also very early because it shows the battlements which have now disappeared.

The use of the castle as a quarry to provide stone for other building in the village is very evident in the local houses and walls, and it is also recorded that stone from the castle was used in building the Trinity Almshouse. Archaeological investigations have shown the presence of several buildings, particularly to the west of the keep, one of which was probably the home of Queen Isabella in the fourteenth century. It would seem that our ancestors forestalled the modern work of the archaeologist by many centuries! Nevertheless I remain puzzled why it is that so much of the keep remains today, in spite of its usefulness as a stone quarry. There are two possible reasons for this. One is that the Howards must have wished to preserve what remained of the buildings which they owned, and the other is that the castle was useful as it was for other purposes. We know that it served as a local gaol, for it seems to have held prisoners awaiting transfer to Swaffham and Norwich Bridewell prisons.

Another reason for its good state of repair may well be the durability of the stone of which it is built, and I shall be saying something about this later. In contrast to our castle, those at New Buckenham and Castle Acre were built of flint, and this material, being irregular in its shape and size may not have lasted so well as our shaped blocks of limestone and sandstone. Professor Brown points out that another storey seems to have been added to the keep, and several traces of the change in the building can be seen. Changes can be seen too above the entrance lobby, where gothic arches have been inserted over the original rounded Norman ones. It was the basement under the entrance lobby which was said to have been used as the local gaol, no doubt under the charge of the Mayor's Sargeant.

The so-called chapel, almost buried under the ramparts on the eastern side of the keep, is of course the oldest building in Rising, and it is difficult to date it with precision. It is generally thought to have been early Norman rather than Saxon in origin. It is not really correct for it to be called a chapel, for it was the Church of Rising, and only ceased to be used as such when the position of the keep with its surrounding ramparts made the building of a new and more imposing building essential. Here too we have been fortunate that its remains have not all been destroyed by the search for building materials. Perhaps they have been protected to a great extent by the ramparts which engulfed them.

The Church of St Lawrence

The story of the new church can, in the virtual absence of early records, only be told by the alterations and additions which have left their mark in the structure. It can be seen for example that the famous west front, that people come from miles away to photograph and which Nicholas Pevsner calls 'swagger', was a later addition by the Norman builders, for the earlier Norman windows of plain design which can be seen from inside the church were filled in to provide the decorated Norman west front.

Another feature that can be seen is the south transept, which is itself a Victorian replacement of an earlier transept, which left its imprint on the south face of the tower where its roof was even higher than the present transept. One can go even further back in time by noticing, from inside the tower, that there used to be two early Norman windows. Very pleasant it must have been to have south-facing windows at this point to give light beneath the tower. A south transept in a church in a village as small as Rising can never have been really necessary. We nearly had the misfortune of a north transept as well, because plans existed in the 1890's to construct one, but these fortunately came to nothing.

The Norfolk County Records Office contains details of two restorations of the church. The first, of 1749, was paid for by Viscount Andover who lived in the Hall at Rising. The rates paid for labour in the church make interesting comparison with those of today.

Carpenters work at Castle Rising Church by Jacob Foreman for making and framing ye church roof, making a new pulpit, and repairing ye pews etc by order of Rich. Fawssett for ye Rt Hon. Viscount Andover:

1749	Aug 5	2 days in church	£0- 3-4
	Aug 11	3 days in church	£0- 5-0
	Aug 19	4 days in church	£0- 6-4
	Aug 26	5 days in church	£0- 8-4
	Sept 2	6 days in church	£0-10-0
	Sept 9	3 days in church	£0- 5-4
	Sept 16	4 days in church	£0- 6-8
	Sept 30	4 days in church	£0- 6-8
	Oct 4	5 days in church	£0- 8-4

Oct 14	a day in church and two days clearing	£0- 5-0
	2 days making the scafolds and helping the weathercock up and taking scafolds down	£0- 3-4
To making and framing roof		£5- 0-0

Decd Nov 4th 1749 of Rich Fawssett eight pounds £8- 8-4
eight shillings in full of the above bill for
carpentry work in repairing Castle Rising Church
Witness Henry Loftus The mark of Jacob Foreman ×

The work must have been the rebuilding of 'the mean embattled tower' of an old description which appears in the Cotman drawing of 1811, and is in my personal view a much more traditional roof than the saddle erected in the 1846-1850 restoration. We are also told that twenty-three tons of lead were laid on the roof during this restoration, the total of which came to £111-14-3d.

Later drawings of the church show that the first saddle roof to the tower of 1846 was raised to the much higher existing level. It is interesting that the saddle roof on the entrance lobby of the castle can be seen in the Buck etching of 1738, and one supposes that the similar roof on the church tower was based on this.

The south side of the church has seen many alterations over the course of years, most of which can be traced either from the remains of earlier features, or from old drawings. The Cotman etching of 1811* shows large rectangular Nave windows set within large, round-arched Norman ones. Also shown is a curiously shaped south-east chapel against the south-east wall of the nave, which must have had a second storey judging from the upward slanting squint which can still be seen above the altar near the Norman arch between the nave and tower.

The Cotman drawing also shows the position of the roof of the first south-facing nave, which is said by Bradfer Lawrence to have been of Henry III date. It makes one realise how many changes must have been made in a building such as this which has been in continual use over the centuries. It makes one realise too what terrible neglect there must have been during the eighteenth

* See illustration no 6

century; for example, Blomefield states in 1800 that the chancel was in ruins.

The Market Cross

The imposing cross in the middle of the Market Green is of sufficient importance to have a paragraph to itself. Taylor does not mention its existence, but Bradfer Lawrence thinks it may have been Norman in date. Nicholas Pevsner on the other hand calls it fifteenth-century in origin. A clue to a more accurate dating may lie in the nature of the stone itself. The Geological Museum in South Kensington consider that it is Barnack limestone, and came from a village of that name in Northamptonshire. It is undoubtedly the same stone as was used for the facings of both the Castle and the Church, and it would have been brought from Barnack by water down one of the rivers that drain into the Wash and landed at the tidal harbour at Rising.

According to the museum, this stone, which was used in the building of many of the great Fenland Abbeys, was exhausted by the end of the fifteenth century, so that the Market Cross could, as Pevsner says, have been built as late as this, but with our knowledge of the decay of the castle after the end of the fourteenth century, it seems very unlikely that a market cross as imposing as this would have been built by the royal owners of the estate at this time. It seems much more likely that it was built at about the same time as the church, and at a time when it lent added importance to the new status of the village which was brought about by the building of the castle.

Naturally it must have been restored from time to time as frost loosened the stones. The last restoration was in 1974, but the hard shelly limestone weathers well, and the blocks are re-used again and again. We are indeed fortunate to have such a fine monument, which must always have lent tone to the village, particularly at times when fairs were held on the Green. It is recorded in the patent rolls that in the year 1254 there was a grant to Roger Monte Alto (Lord Roger de Montalt, the baron who married Cecily d'Albini) and to his heirs, of a fair at Rising on the eve of Ascension Day and the fourteen days following. Ascension Day is one of those moveable feasts which depend on the date of Easter, and according to the Book of Common Prayer, it can fall on any day between 30 April to 3 June.

Trinity Hospital

The Hospital was built in 1609-15 at a cost of £451 by Henry Howard, Earl of Northampton, who was a younger brother of Thomas, the fourth Duke of Norfolk who lost his head in 1572. This was an age when it was not uncommon to found charitable institutions, and he built another almshouse at Clun in Shropshire, and one at Greenwich. It is unlikely that he built it because he felt that his sins were worse than other men. He was a Catholic, and with Elizabeth I on the throne, anyone who belonged to the other brand of Christianity would have been considered suspect. It was said of him that he was one of the most unscrupulus and treacherous characters of his age, but on the other hand that he was distinguished for his learning, artistic culture and public character. One feels that his reputation owes more to the fashionable habits of the period of vilifying anyone who belonged to the religious party which was not in power.

In his will, which was written in his own hand, he says "I will that myne heir forever shall have the placinge and displacinge and nominacioun of the pore of the Hospitall of Rising". The word 'Hospital' is at least as old as 'Almshouse' and, to quote the *Oxford Dictionary*, is 'a charitable institution for the housing and maintenance of the needy, infirm and aged'. Rising Hospital was founded for women, and according to the statutes 'They must be of honest life and conversation, religious, grave and discreet, able to read, if such a one be had, a single woman, her place to be void on marriage, to be fifty six years of age at least, no common beggar, harlot, scold, drunkard, haunter of taverns, inns and alehouses.'

The pensioners wear attractive bright red cloaks bearing the Howard Arms on special occasions such as Founder's Day and on going to church on Sundays, but the tall conical hats of an earlier period are no longer popular, and have been replaced by black hats of more modern appearance. The Matron of the Hospital wears a hat of a different style.

The building, of warm red brick made in the parish, is sometimes called Elizabethan, but as it was not started until 1609, it could more properly be called Jacobean. It remains in almost the same condition in which it was built, although the provision of bathrooms for the inmates has reduced their number from the original twelve to nine. It is now governed by the Mercers Company of London, with a board of trustees most of whom are local people.

THE EIGHTEENTH-CENTURY VILLAGE

The Howard owners and their Agents

We have now taken the story of Rising from the time of the building of the Castle to the purchase of the Rising Estate including the considerable lands in the Woottons, Gaywood, Roydon and Congham by another branch of the Howard family – Thomas Howard of Ashstead Manor in Surrey. He must have been quite wealthy because he was a Teller of the Exchequer, and son and heir of Sir Robert Howard who had been Auditor of the Exchequer. You will notice a number of names of people appearing in our story from time to time, who were mostly different members of the Howard family. For example, a Howard who commissioned a map of the estate which has been of the greatest service in sorting out the history of the village was the Earl of Berkshire, he was the heir of Thomas Howard of Ashstead. The Earl of Suffolk also succeeded at a slightly later time as did Viscount Andover – I mention the names not to try and demonstrate the family succession, which is pretty complicated, but to show that these Howards seem to have been really interested in the estate, as opposed to the various Dukes of Norfolk, who apart from their unfortunate propensity for backing the wrong side, and having their heads chopped off in the process, were the possessors of such huge territories that an estate of some 5,000 acres such as the Manor of Rising Chase, could rarely if ever have been visited by them.

Thomas Howard was an absentee landlord in just the same way as were his royal predecessors, and even to a great extent the d'Albini's and the Montalts. Most landowners travelled the countryside visiting their various properties, staying for a period at each to transact necessary business. Thomas's main seat was Ashstead Park, but he also had estates at Elford in Staffordshire, and at Levens in Westmoreland. He managed his estates through an agent, who was a man of some standing and importance in the neighbourhood, perhaps a solicitor or someone of that status, and it is to the preservation of the letters written by the agent that we owe so many interesting details of life in the village. In representing the Lord of the Manor, it generally fell to his lot to swear in the Mayor, and generally to attend to the affairs of the estate.

The letters from the owner to the agent have rarely survived, but we get a good idea of what went on from the agents' letters, and it is greatly to the credit of the lord that the estate papers have been so well preserved. These are now in the safe keeping of the County Record Office at Norwich where they may be studied. It is nevertheless not easy to obtain a connected story and a number of blanks in our knowledge remain to tantalise us and to make us wish that we knew the answers to many questions which must have been perfectly well known to our village ancestors.

For example. I would much like to know the year of the building of the Mansion House, which later became known as The Hall. I live in a house which used to be an adjunct of this old building, and I know that it was in existence in 1742 because a description of it appears in early records, as well as an inventory of Lord Andover's furniture and effects.

The Hall consisted of a great room or hall, a parlour and servants' hall and no doubt a few other rooms. An interesting inventory exists of the bedding which reads as follows:

> '11 feather beds, 11 bolsters, 17 pillows, 17 blankets, three very bad quilts.' [with a note in another hand saying worn out and eaten with moths].

From the above there may have been about half a dozen bedrooms, and it was noted as being the property of Viscount and Viscountess Andover, the Howard owner of that time, but the poor state of the bedding indicates that the house was seldom lived in, and in fact this is mentioned in more than one record, as in one set of estate accounts where no rental was shown for the Hall, it being unoccupied. On another occasion the agent offered the hospitality of his own house at Wisbech during the owner's stay in the district.

In later years the only other resident of note was Lord Farquhar, with whom King Edward VII used to stay when he was Prince of Wales. It was while he was up here for the shooting that he found

Sandringham, which was purchased by Queen Victoria. The Hall survived until after the Second World War, and its last use seems to have been the housing of evacuees from the dockland area of London in 1940. A couple of years ago I was surprised to see four ladies looking in a puzzled fashion at my house, and wondering where was the house they remembered as child evacuees, and which they had come all the way from London to see! From what they told me the Hall 'had lovely large rooms' and they had the happiest memories of their war-time visit. I have heard from older residents that their mothers were known as the dancing housewives of Castle Rising, by reason of the fact that they took their leisure in the evenings when their children were safely tucked up in bed!

It is time now to take a look at the village in the last three centuries, its layout, its houses and its life.

The Village Layout

There is a little doggerel rhyme which was quoted by William Taylor in his book which must be repeated here if only to dispute the view it expresses that Rising was once a seaport town of importance.

> 'Rising was a seaport town, when Lynn was but a marsh.
> Now Lynn it is a seaport town, and Rising fares the worse.'

This of course is complete nonsense, for there is no evidence at all that Rising was ever any more in its harbour facilities than Brancaster is today. It would have been most unlikely in any case that a settlement on the modest-sized Babingly river could ever have compared with the Ouse, which is one of the major rivers of the country which drains several counties.

The map of 1588 already mentioned, shows Lynn to have been a seaport and a monastic town, with houses, warehouses, churches and monasteries all tightly packed together within its mediaeval defensive wall, which had little connection with the countryside. It was bounded on the south and west by large areas of fen and marsh which were very thinly populated, whereas Rising hemmed it in on the east and north and was itself the centre of what was known from very early times as the Chase, and which included Gaywood, Grimston and the Woottons.

There was no reason to suppose that Rising was ever more than a small village except when the Normans came and selected it as the site for their west Norfolk castle. At times it would no doubt have had a number of retainers based on the castle, but these would have been a moveable population who would have travelled about with their lord and his lady between their different establishments. The Chase itself consisted of a well-wooded agricultural area with fields of highly variable fertility owing to the big differences in the nature of the soil. One field would have been barren sand and gravel, another chalk with flints, and right next door to them a patch of heavy clay derived from the effects of the last ice age, and in the valley of the Babingley rich soil but much subject to flooding at times of gale and high tide.

Some areas were no doubt suited to woodland and forest which is the case today, and this must have favoured the game for which it is still noted. The valley of the Babingley river which bounds the parish to the north is now a fertile plain, but until the sea wall was pushed out to the west and built to a height which resisted the ravages of the high tides, there was always a battle to maintain the fertility of the land. In mediaeval times the area was ideal for the production of salt by the evaporation of sea water, and this was an industry which flourished all round the Wash. Traces still exist of salt pans which used to be constructed at the high water mark. The river had a staithe, and small ships worked up to the harbour until about 1690, when it was closed by a sluice gate, shown on the early maps.

The Howards as was the custom of many landlords of the time, caused maps to be prepared which they needed for the general management of the estate, and we are fortunate that the County Record Office contains a number of these which give quite a good idea of the village as it was in the seventeenth and later centuries. They are sometimes quite large, that of 1732 being about ten feet by six, and this was necessary to illustrate the fields of the farms which spread from the salt marsh in the west to the parishes of Congham and Roydon in the east.

This has the result of reducing the area occupied by the settlement itself to quite a small area, and in one or two cases the folding of the map – by ill fortune just on the village area – has resulted in scuffing of the surface which makes it very difficult to decipher.

I made a tracing of the roads and houses to obtain an idea of the roads and pathways which is illustrated here.* It was bad luck that the map of 1732 which illustrated the road system in use when the harbour was in existence, was the one worst affected by wear and the former building which housed the Black Horse for example is illegible, but this does not really affect the usefulness of the map.

It can be seen that there are many short cuts in the village which enabled the inhabitants to get from one place to another by the most direct route. For example Nightmarsh Lane continued past the cottages to the south to give direct access to the Market Green. A north-south road went by the west side of the Mansion House and connected the Green with Lynn Road.

The most important difference however was the existence of two roads which do not exist today, one called Havengate Lane which was a continuation of the road leading north from the Green to the old harbour. The other one was an east to west road which ran parallel with and about twenty yards north of the existing Lower road. Its position is marked by the existence of several houses set well back from the lower road, of which one is the ruined pair of cottages in Nightmarsh Lane. The existing lower road used to continue to the west to serve the cottages at the west end of the village and joined up with the road to Lynn some 200 yards from the existing outlet.

Blomefield's *Norfolk* of 1805 says of Havengate Lane 'It is very oozy, and in this lane there was some years past in digging up, found a piece of an anchor belonging to some ship'. Mention is made in other records of Seagate Lane, Black Lane and Pudding Lane, but they were not marked on any map and it is difficult to identify them with any certainty. The Old Parsonage house was in Seagate Lane, but as the 1732 map shows it to have been built on the site of the present Rectory (built in 1809), it would seem pretty certain that Seagate Lane was what we now call the old Hunstanton road. Pudding Lane was near Nightmarsh Lane, and this may have been the name given to one of the two parallel lower roads.

There is no evidence of any buildings on the site of the old harbour, and there seems no doubt that the harbour consisted merely of a staithe or landing stage alongside which vessels could tie up when the tide was high. We shall see later that floods at times of spring tide as well as tidal surges caused by the wind would

* inside back cover illustration.

always have caused flooding in such places as Nightmarsh Lane, and the position of the most northerly houses would have been dictated by the height to which the highest tides normally rose.

As one would expect, the Marsh figures prominently in the field names. Court Marsh was one, but mostly they were identified by reference to other named fields, for example the Sedgy Marsh adjoining the old sluice, or all that salt marsh lying from Rising Marys to the old sluice. There were also of course the Night Marsh and the Day Marsh which in those days were common land for the use of the inhabitants.

Some of the field names are rather charming. There are a number of Brecks or Brakes such as Mustard Seed Brake or Spring Brake, a number of Closes such as Cromers Close or Great and Little Gayton's Close and Malthouse Close. A number of Car's such as Alder Car, the Car Lands, and most important from the viewpoint of history, the Mayor's Car, a field of about ten acres which was one of the rewards for undertaking the often quite onerous job of Mayor of the Borough of Rising. The Pightles were quite numerous at certain times, for example the Parson's Pightle (pronounced pie-tle). The Pightles were the early vegetable gardens, of which more later. Other field names were Great and Little Hog Marys, Fishpool Hill, Bullard's Hill, and there was the curious name of Goos Moor for the common land now called Castle Rising Wood on the north side of the road to Hillington. My favourite name is Paradice for the three and a half acre field at the bottom and to the west of Nightmarsh Lane.

The Houses

It is not easy to make precise statements about the size of the village in former centuries, other than to say that it was never very different from what it is today, that is to say before the new houses of 1975 and later years were erected. No doubt there were a fair number of retainers employed at the castle in the early days, but we are dealing here with the period since 1693, and the earliest map, that of 1588, seems to show from thirty-three to thirty-six dwellings, depending on how one interprets the little three-dimensional drawings which look rather like the little wooden blocks used in the game of Monopoly.

The next map, that of 1732, is accompanied by a schedule which lists thirty-four 'tenements', many of which consisted of double cottages, and a few, as is the case today, built to house three or more families. The Tithe Map of 1838 is also accompanied with a schedule from which one may see that sixty-one households were listed, and this can fairly be compared with the number of sixty to sixty-one households whose tenements qualified them or rather their occupier, for a vote in parliamentary elections from 1693 onwards until the rotten boroughs were abolished (Castle Rising was one of these).

From a careful examination of the map of 1732 it is possible to ascertain with a fair degree of accuracy that some fifteen of the thirty-four dwellings, which were called 'tenements' in an accompanying list, still exist today. My calculation must be tentative because the prime purpose of the map was to show the boundaries of the fields, and as the centre of the map which showed the village itself was very worn, it is difficult to distinguish buildings in the centre of the village. As carrstone, although it is durable, is quite easy to rebuild and repair, the precise age of a house is difficult to determine. There is no problem with the houses of the 1840-50 period because these have common features and are often dated anyway, but dating is more difficult earlier than this.

At this time the Castle had lost its early importance although it was a favourite subject for artists, and we have many pictures of it as a ruin with trees and shrubs growing out of it.

It is possible that the castle provided a lodging for the Mayor's sargeant, but the wooden floors of the keep would long since have rotted away, and only the stone floored rooms in the entrance lobby would have provided shelter.

The Hospital was finished in 1615, and Bradfer Lawrence says that there was a Guildhall on the south-west corner of the Green which was owned by the Mayors, but which was purchased by Henry Howard, Earl of Northampton, in 1604. The Parsonage House was replaced by the rectory in 1809 when the Rev Richard Fawssett, a member of the same family who provided an agent for the Howard estate, decided to build a more worthy residence on the site of the old house.

Another building in the village which is of considerable age is the large tiled barn which is part of the complex of buildings which made up Castle Farm, but whether this was the same farm as the 'demesne' mentioned in Domesday we do not know. The western face of the barn contains a good variety of stones rather similar to

1. *Castle Rising Castle in 1738 by S. M. Buck*

2. *Castle Rising Castle by Millicent, showing Isabella's lodging in the foreground (date not known)*

3. *The East Window in Castle Rising Church*
Etching by J. S. Cotman

4. *The Entrance to the Keep*
Etching by J. S. Cotman

5. *The eleventh-century church in the grounds of the Castle by William Taylor*

6. *The church at Castle Rising in 1811*
Etching by J. S. Cotman

7. The church at Castle Rising in 1849
William Taylor

8. The font in Castle Rising church – probably moved from the Castle church
Etching by J. S. Cotman

9. *An interior view of the church before the installation of the pews and pulpit in 1849. Artist unknown*

10. *The Hall – pulled down in the 1950s*

11. *Almswomen by Miss Goodwin, 1849*

12. *Portrait of a Lady (possibly Catherine Howard). Artist unknown*
By kind permission of H.M. the Queen

the west end of one of the buildings of the former Black Horse. The latter moved to its present site in late Victorian days. It used to have stabling for five horses and was one of the most important of the licensed houses in the village. There was another farm situated on the lower road, but only one wall of its barn remains, and this contains yet another type of building stone – clunch, a hard chalk used quite a lot in the district. This tiled barn can be seen in a charming watercolour of 1849 painted by F. C. Lukis from just within the west door of the Church, which can be seen at the Castle Museum at Norwich. Other buildings of this, now the Home Farm, still remain.

No talk about the houses in the village would be complete without a description of the materials from which they were built. The village is well supplied with local stone, having not only a plentiful supply of carrstone, which is easily worked and quite durable, but also it had and still has blocks or boulders of grey coloured sandstone, which are found lying about on the surface in several parts of the parish. These are part of the Sandringham sand formation which has been extensively mined at Leziate, and the stone occurs where the surface of the sand has been affected by streams which have carried silica into it and have hardened it into a durable stone. A lot has been used in the building of the church and the castle, and the walls of the former can be seen to contain large boulders of it.

Only one house is built of the grey Sandringham sandstone, although there are several at Hillington built from this material. The rest are built from the carrstone which occurred plentifully nearby, with door and window surrounds made from the local brick. There was a piece of land near the harbour called the Brick Ground, and the bricks have a lovely russet to dark red appearance and of course vary in colour according to their degree of firing. One of the walls surrounding the old Castle farm are built of this brick, and it has a most attractive appearance.

An interesting comment on the wearing qualities of the carrstone occurs in a letter from the agent James Bellamy to the Lord of the Manor when writing of the building of the village school in 1813.

Honourable Sir,

You did not mention whether the building was to be formed of brick or stone, but I presume the latter, to be faced in the same manner as the wall in the garden at Castle Rising, which I think is very neat. It is less expensive and stronger than brick....

How things have changed in modern times, for few craftsmen are trained to work in the stone, although it cuts very easily and, as James Bellamy says, has got very good wearing qualities.

House walls are often very thick, and in my own house consist of an outer and an inner skin of stone with a rubble filling which allows the passage of air just as if it was a cavity wall. Perhaps it is this which keeps our houses so free of damp. I had not realised until I came to know Rising well, how attractive was the rough and varied texture of the walls and houses, particularly the older ones in which one can find three or four different types of building material. One wonders what a modern planning committee would do if one were to submit an application for building a house with so many varied materials! The bits I like are the old doorways which have been blocked up in times past with surprising bits of stone and brickbats – if only they could speak, what tales they could tell! Much of this varied material came from old buildings, especially the castle.

A feature of the use of carrstone as a building material is the little pieces of stone that are pressed into the mortar joints between the stones.* Various reasons have been suggested for these, of which the most intriguing was that they were inserted to keep the witches away. I don't know that I have ever seen a witch in the village, at any rate one with a broomstick, but one never knows. Once when digging round the foot of a big yew tree in my garden, I came across a cache of strange bones, and here again local opinion was that these were buried to keep the witches away. Speaking purely for myself, I don't know that I really want them kept away, and I have wondered what would happen if I were to dig them up and send them away in the dustcart.

One is often asked about the age of the houses in the village. I have already said that one can trace that fifteen of the houses were in existence in 1732, and it is quite possible that some of them are much earlier than this. In considering this question one must remember that they were probably nearly all built and maintained by the estate itself, for the agent had a number of men on his payroll, carpenters, masons and so on. One document records that a

* Known as Galleting.

great gale in 1833 did great damage on the estate, and several vessels were wrecked on the salt marsh. In a letter to Col. Howard at Ashstead the agent says

> 'a great quantity of wreckage is strewn along the saltings all of which I have desired to be carried to the carpenters shop. There are two boats belonging to vessels sunk in the channel, I have written to say that they may be had by the proper authorities. Three vessels are stranded, two of which I think may be got off, the other I fear must be broken up, with your permission. . . . Another vessel is visible at low water which I have desired Smith to break up and take to the carpenters shop. . . .'

It would seem that not all was a loss to the estate, and in doing some repairs in the bell chamber of the church it was clear to me that the heavy timbers of the bell cage had once seen service at sea!

The octagonal chimneys which we see on so many of the houses seem to date from the 1850's, and this can be deduced from the fact that two or three of the houses with these chimneys have a plate recording that they were built by Mary Howard at this time. But other houses have them which we know existed in 1732, so one may assume that the estate builders who specialised in these handsome chimneys used them as a standard replacement whenever a chimney needed rebuilding.

It is rather sad that fashion and economic pressures have caused so much building in the village to be of brick, and this is often of a type and colour which is quite foreign to what has been used in the village for hundreds of years. The carrstone is quite easily available and with modern stone cutting equipment can easily be cut to any convenient site, as is done in the Costwolds and other stone-producing areas. One finds it difficult to accept that the argument of high cost should be allowed to upset the building habits of centuries, especially when one knows that no serious attempt has been made to work the stone with modern tools.

THE PEOPLE

The real life of the village was concerned with its people, and in these days when most of those who live in the village work outside it, it is difficult to imagine the sort of place it was even a hundred years ago, for most of the villagers worked and earned their living within the parish, and everyone was interested in the business of his neighbour. Men and women walked to their work perhaps from Nightmarsh Lane to Lodge Farm on Knight's Hill, or from Havengate Lane to work in the corn mill on the Babingley river.

The impression one gets from studying the old maps and records is that there were few walls and fences in the village, although there must have been paling fences to keep straying animals from enjoying the vegetables grown in the pightles round the cottages, but nevertheless there was plenty of space between one property and another, to allow free passage almost in a straight line from one point to another. For example there were pathways on either side of the church to the Market Green, in fact one could have walked on to the Green from almost any direction.

The Market Green is now the personal property of the lord of the manor, and permission has to be sought before it can be used by those who live in the village. One of the most extraordinary and unjust Acts ever passed by Parliament was that which allowed the use or sale of the common lands for the personal gain of the hereditary owner. Our own Market Green had a road driven over it as late as 1974, and the Howard papers at Norwich contain a notice or handbill which advertises the sale of the Common lands at Congham, an adjoining village, on 7 July 1813. Five lots were for sale including the Great Common and the Low Common. Such misuses of land which had been preserved for hundreds of years for the benefit of local people, are one of the great stains on the record of the hereditary owners. It is a mercy that the footpath rights have been preserved, and these at least can be enjoyed by the modern inhabitants of the parish.

But to return to the past, when a man or a woman had finished their work on the farm or the mill or the brickworks, you would find them in one of two places – their homes or their pub. Yes, their pub – for at one time as we shall see there were half a dozen to choose from, of which only the Black Horse is with us today. Some of them must have been very small and decrepit places, and it is difficult to imagine how they could have afforded a living to their tenants, but they existed and in the days when there was no cinema or other place of entertainment, they were literally the only places where people could met and talk and relax after their day's work in various parts of the parish.

On Sunday, a man and his wife would have gone to church, and his attendance was expected there unless there was a good excuse for his absence such as illness or essential work. Life in the village revolved around three people – the lord of the manor, who owned most of the land and who was directly or indirectly responsible for the earning capacity of the village. Then there was the mayor who was responsible for law and order and had a wide range of duties and responsibilities. Lastly there was the parson, who was responsible for the welfare of the population and particularly for their souls, and this had a much wider meaning in the early days than we can ever imagine today.

I am going to say something of each of these people, and a fourth one, too, will come into the story – the lord of the manor's agent. The Howards were absentee landlords, and it is because of this that we have such a good record of the past, for many of the agent's letters to his master have survived to tell the story.

The Rising Chase Estate

While the village of Rising was a parish in its own right, the estate stretched over several parishes and was called the Chase or the Chace which indicates that originally it was a hunting estate which incorporated several parishes, and it was over this extensive area that the agent ruled on behalf of his master.

When the d'Albinis built their castle at Rising they undoubtedly lived in it when they visited their Norfolk estates, as did their successors the Montalts, but they owned huge tracts of land and they cannot have stayed at Rising for long periods, and in this sense they were absentee landlords as were the royal owners who came after them. Of the latter only Edward III came to Rising on several visits to see his mother Queen Isabella. When Henry VIII gave the manor to the Duke of Norfolk, it was only one of several estates owned by the Duke, so that it would seldom have been visited by its ducal owners. We will start with a dramatic story told by James Bellamy who was Richard Howard's agent in a letter dated 24 April 1798.

He reported that his predecessor Thomas Fawssett met his death when his carriage was returning from a visit to Outwell. It was crossing a river when the horses took fright and the carriage overturned into the river, and Mr Fawssett was drowned. Bellamy must have been a close connection, for in the same letter he applied for the vacant place, and his application seems to have been granted. He remained the Howard agent for twenty-nine years. He lived not at Rising but at Wisbech, and no doubt managed other estates as well as that of Rising.

Many of his letters to Ashstead were purely routine, and dealt with such matters of the letting of the corn mill to a new tenant, and included detailed lists of the fittings, such as cogwheels, water wheels, sluices and so on. At other times it was the state of the crops which claimed attention. In a letter in July 1805 he said 'I never saw the crops look better in Norfolk than at present'; but in February 1809 'I never saw so much water on the low lands at Rising and Babingley. . . .' Let us hope that things dried up before the summer. Rising was by no means the only village to depend on the crops for its living, for a good harvest meant relative prosperity for the local farmers, and no famine in the following winter.

The main village activity has always been farming, and the farms were let by the Howard estate to various tenants at rents which in 1799 for example produced the following income for the estate:

Castle Rising	£642- 1-6d.
North Wootton	£1002-15-6d.
Roydon and Congham	£318- 7-0d.
Gaywood	£17- 5-0d.
Total	£1980- 9-0d.

With the addition of quit rents and casual profits the total was

£2033-10-4d. from which expenses of £350 and Land Tax of £74 had to be deducted, giving a net income from some 2071 acres of farm land of about £1500 – not a bad income for those days.

The Floods

Things cannot always have been as good, because there were demands from farmers for a reduction in rent when their land was badly affected by storm and tempest. I have already mentioned the bad storm of 1833, and this was not the only one to cause loss and damage in the parish, and there were several occasions when the low lands were affected by high tides. One such occurred in 1781, and is worth quoting at some length:

> My Lady Oct 31 1781
>
> After a favourable prospect of the state of your concerns in Norfolk, it is now an unpleasing task to trouble you with a very different Picture. I went to Castle Rising last Sunday sennight, and the next day did the business of swearing into office the Mayor elect, much to my satisfaction But that satisfaction was counterbalanced by the dismal effects of a very unexpected tide which happened the Friday before, about seven in the morning, and tho' there was very little Wind overflow'd all the Banks.
>
> All the marsh lands rented by my brother Oliver (the new tenant who succeeded the Widows) Standbanks and other tenants, were covered with sea water two or three feet deep. My brother was fortunately in the Marshes very early in the morning, and saw the approaching danger soon enough to get all his sheep off the Lands, or they must have been lost. The neighbours were alarmed, so that providentially their cattle were all saved. My Brother had sown 25 acres of wheat which he thinks is destroyed. There is a general murmuring among the Tenants, and had not the Banks (which Mr Carter saw) been in exceeding good condition the misfortune must have been much aggravated. The Land side of the Banks by the overflowing of the Tide water is much damaged, but there is no breach thro' any part of these Banks. I do not look upon the damage of the Banks as the greatest misfortune. The Lands will be materially injured, the Tenants distressed for keeping for their cattle, and so frequent a succession of these accidents which no human care or foresight can prevent, will deter any man from venturing his property in

such a situation.

I have given directions for the immediate repair of the Banks, which were higher and in better condition than the adjacent Banks, which shared the same fate. I shall be glad to be favoured with your Ladyship's sentiments and directions in the matters, which will govern the conduct of your Obedient and faithful Ser.[t]

and humble Ser.[t]
Thomas Fawssett

The Lady to whom Thomas Fawssett was writing was the Hon Frances Howard, who married Richard Bagot, who afterwards changed his name to Howard. The agent's letters are a mine of information, and not always on such gloomy matters as gales and floods. One letter of December 1828 is full of interesting pieces of information. It is written by another agent, William Newton. Here are some extracts from it.

> 'I have given the necessary directions respecting planting out the trees in the Nursery and Garden as you desired; Vine has sent me word that all the plants you sent from Elford arrived in perfect condition, and they have all been carefully laid in the ground and properly protected.... The new fence on the Common next the Car is raised, and I propose to continue it thro' the Glebe Land if it meets your approbation (I have obtained Rev Broderick's consent)... May I beg the favour to inform me whether you wish the piece of land formerly part of an old lane adjoining the Lawn in front of the Mansion to be planted. . . . Two men are employed in sifting the rubbish in the Castle Yard already raised, and I beg to know whether you would wish the whole to be raised and sifted on the South side of the Castle (leaving all the foundations of any buildings) or whether you would prefer an opening to be made at the south west corner of the Castle by the well and to continue the quarry at the back of the Castle between that and the embankment. . . . I remain dear Sir, most respectfully, your very obliged humble servant Wm Newton.

I took an opportunity of showing a copy of this letter to the Ministry of Works Archaeologist who was excavating at the castle, and I could not help wondering whether William Newton had left him anything worth finding some 150 years later!

The Desperate Gang of Villains

There were worrying times for the people of Rising as is shown in a letter of 1813.

> Honourable Sir,
> I have the satisfaction of informing you that a desperate gang of villains in this neighbourhood have been discovered and sent to Norwich Castle. They resided at Congham, Grimston and other places and were the terror of the neighbourhood. Eight of them are now secured, and strict search is making after two or three others who have absconded.

In a later letter the agent is able to report '. . . I have caused several since the late dispute to be sent to Swaffam Bridewell where they have been properly received'.

It appears that Bridewell was a former royal lodging in London which Edward VI gave for use as a hospital, and which was later used as a house of correction. The name derived from St Bride's Well, became to be generally used and applied to a prison. This reminds me of another letter of 1813 in which the Borough of Rising prosecuted the head Jailer of Norwich Bridewell for allowing a Castle Rising prisoner to escape! There is quite a lot of correspondence which does not seem to arrive at any definite conclusion, and I suspect from something that was said, that the trouble arose because the Borough of Rising failed to pay rates due at Norwich for the housing of prisoners!

Rising went through quite a bad bit of trouble in 1830 and a letter from Frederick Lane the agent gives news of it to his master:

> The Honourable Col Howard — Lynn 30 Novr. 1830
> Ashstead
> Dear Sir,
>
> The tumultuous Proceedings of certain classes having extended to this neighbourhood, I am anxious that no exertions should be wanting on our part to afford to the Inhabitants of the several Parishes within the Castle Rising Jurisdiction, that Protection that the Laws provide and with this view I have con-

ferred with Mr Freeman upon the propriety of increasing the Constabulary Force. Mr Freeman is very ready to do all in his power to meet the exigency of the case, and it has occurred to us that great benefits may result from the employment of a Night Watch to guard against the designs of the Incendiaries. As this system cannot be carried out without an additional expenditure, I take the liberty of inquiring whether you will authorise me to add your name to any Fund that may be subscribed for Castle Rising and the adjoining Parishes, to meet the present emergency and to what extent.

I regret to say that fresh instances occur daily of fresh acts of insubordination and outrage, but I trust the native labourers are as yet free from stain of originating the tumult.

I am, dear Sir, Your truly obliged and faithful
servant Fred. Lane

Education and the Relief of the Poor

As so often happens, we do not know the end of the story, and one supposes that Colonel Howard paid up and no further letter was necessary. The riots of 1830 were symptomatic of those which occurred all over the country, and which were due to the low level of wages at that time and the constant struggle to exist. These in turn were due to the state of depression in agriculture, the operation of the Corn Laws and a host of other factors into which it is not possible to enter here.

It is however pertinent to quote what Sir James Caird said in his *English Agriculture* published in 1851, of the diet of the typical labourer on Salisbury Plain. This area fell within the area of the country in which wages were as low as an average of 7/- per week, an area which included Norfolk.

> We were curious to see how the money was economised, and heard from a labourer the following account of a day's diet. After doing up his horses he takes breakfast, which is made of flour with a little butter, and water from the teakettle poured over it. He takes with him to the field a piece of bread and (if he has not a young family and can afford it) cheese to eat at mid-day. He returns home in the afternoon to a few potatoes, and possibly a little bacon, although only those who are better off can afford this. The supper very commonly consists of bread and

> water. The appearance of the labourer showed, as might be expected from such meagre diet, a want of that vigour and activity which marks the well fed ploughman of the northern and midland counties. Beer is given by the master in haytime and harvest. Some farmers allow ground for planting potatoes to their labourers, and carry home their fuel – which on the downs, where there is no wood, is a very expensive article in a labourer's family.

There is no reason to suppose that Rising had a higher standard of living than that described above, although conditions may well have been better, for the records show that free distributions of food were made by the estate to those in need, and there is every reason to think that the Howards behaved responsibly to the tenants. In one letter the agent refers to the provision made for the poor in Rising, and says

> 'I believe that the poor in Castle Rising are more comfortably provided for than in most of the villages in Norfolk, and there is no defect in police within the Borough . . . the new school is well filled, and there is every reason to think that its good effects will in time be visible in the morals of the rising generation.'

Incidentally the correspondence about the building of the school shows that the agent only dissuaded his master with some difficulty from building the school on the Market Green; he suggested its present site as being suitable, which is a blessing to us modern residents!

It was abundantly clear that whenever the village needed something, it was the lord of the manor who was expected to provide it. When floods devastated the land it was the lord who had to pay by reducing rents; when gales stripped off the pantiles from a tenant's house it was the lord who had to replace them. It is no surprise therefore that when it was felt that something had to be done to educate the children of the village, it was the lord who had to provide both the building and the land on which to build it.

The Mad and Frantic Miller of Rising

This account of the part played by the lord of the manor and his agent in the life of the village does not set out to be a complete one. One could have said so much more; perhaps of the draining of the marsh and the building of the present sea wall in 1840, of the coming of the railway in 1901, or of the recurrent bouts of fever which used to attack the people – could it have been due to the surface wells from which the people drew their water? But just one more story must be told – that of the Mad and Frantic Miller of Castle Rising.

It appears that in 1746 the agent Richard Fawssett was sorely tried by one John Parrott who was the tenant of the Fulling Mill. This was the mill upstream of the old corn mill, whose ruins are still there today. In most beautiful copper plate writing the agent, Richard Fawssett, on 30 August 1746 wrote to his master a defence of all his actions in his dealings with the tenant of the mill whereon, he says, a Fulling Mill formerly stood. He had advanced some £300 to John Parrot to reconstruct the mill to a Paper Mill, and this mill went into production, but alas with recriminations on either side as to the performance of the repayment of the moneys advanced. Having made what appears to be a very fair case in support of his point of view, he then includes a paragraph describing Parrott as the 'mad and frantic Miller' which shows that the job of being agent to the estate was not always a bed of roses!

> And upon the occasion I must now beg leave to tell your Lordship that I have very great reason to complain of this man's behaviour and ill treatment not only in propagating these false and scandalous Aspersions and abusing me wherever he goes But also in the Great trouble he gives me to pay their rents. But he did not come near me, and whenever I go ask him for the rent he is full of complaints but will hear no reason. His son a Paper maker a sober and industrious young man told me that if his father would let him manage the business could maintain the family well and save money, but he believed they should all be ruined by his father for the Mill was so much out of repair that they could not do half the work they otherwise should. But he is so much altered since the Fit of Illness that he has become the worst tenant upon your Lordship's Estate, But in consideration of his Distemper, And in Pity for his Family, I have always hitherto born with his ill treatment and for Fear of adding to the Poor Wretch's Affliction which is as inconsistent with my Dis-

> position as possible. His poor wife has told me several Times crying that she is weary of her life he is so mad and frantick in the family and his son lately went away from him for the same reason.

Alas there is no conclusion to the story of the Mad and Frantick Miller of Castle Rising, for there is no record of the reply of William Howard Viscount Andover. As Richard Fawsett continued in the office of agent, it is reasonable to suppose that he worked out a solution to his problem of his mad and frantick tenant – or perhaps death mercifully removed him from the paper mill.

The Borough of Castle Rising

Some explanation is needed as to why Rising was a Borough. The word Borough is very ancient, and has a number of meanings. It was used equally to denote a fortress or castle, a town possessing a municipal corporation, or any place larger than a village. Rising qualified on several counts for the title of Borough, and to the above reasons one can add the ancient right it possessed to strike coins, and its right to hold a market. But the word 'Borough' came to have other meanings than this, and an old expression 'to buy a borough' meant to buy the power of controlling the election of a member of Parliament for a borough, and the words 'a rotten borough' meant a borough which had so decayed from its original importance as no longer to be a real constituency.

Rising became a Borough in 1558 and sent two members to Parliament, one of the best known of whom was Samuel Pepys. Only sixty votes, possessed by the owners of land and of burgage tenements, decided who was to be elected, and the effect of this was that any absent owners of premises that carried a vote were encouraged to descend on the village at times of election, where they were feasted and entertained by the rival factions to gain their vote in the election.

There is little doubt that the money disbursed must have had quite a big effect on the life of the village, and the Howard records show several examples of the cost to the estate of meeting the expenses of an election. We get a good idea of what went on from the following list of expenses in the election on 12 January 1688.

To the Ringers	£0-10-00
To the Fidlers	£0-10-00
To the Trumpeters	£0-02- 6
To the Drummers	£0-05-00
for Carring the Maior	£0-10-00
To the serjant	£0-10-00
To the Sexton	£0-02-6
To the Holbertmen	£0-05-00
for Carring the Burgesses	£2-00-00
Messengers and Horse hire	£0-05-00
To the servants	£1-00-00
To six Ale Houses	£12-00-00
To Mr Charles Turner	£5-07-06
The Butchers Bill	£4-10-00
Mr Cases for Wine	£3-12-00
Mr Paynes Sile*	£0-12-00
John Costens Sile	£0-12-00
Nich Collins bill	£2-18-06
Two Barrels of Ale	£2-08-00
for ye flaggmen or Mobbelie sile	£2-08-00
given to ye Hospitall	£0-10-00
	£40-18-00

Underneath is a note of some interest

bills delivered by ye six alehouse keepers which they drew without order of which I have paid them 40s. each as above

Anne Haten widdow	£7-01-03
Sam Rendall	£5-18-10
Robte Chamberlyn	£6-06-00
Sam Cornet	£7-00-06
Symon Villers	£5-01-04
John Costens	£4-18-00

Not the least interesting item here is the fact that at this time there were no less than six pubs in the village. I wish the agent had mentioned their names. The total cost of £40-18-0 is only a small part of the total cost of the election, as can be seen from figures

* Sile was probably the local name for herring.

which Bradfer Lawrence gives of the expenses incurred by the estate in the election of 1708, when they paid £162-4-5½d to bring up a party of electors from London. The party set out on 30 April in that year and did not get back to London until the third week in May. No doubt a good time was had by all, for they refreshed themselves at Brandon and Newmarket, and what they drank and ate when they were in Rising must be one reason for the existence of six pubs!

One reason for the election activity at Rising at about this time was the political rise of the Walpoles at Houghton, one of whom, Robert, was later to become Prime Minister. They were an enterprising and energetic family, and it would appear that Castle Rising was one of the stepping stones that they used to achieve the family representation in Parliament. Quite a good proportion of the properties in and around Rising were owned by the Walpoles* and other families, and the reason for this was that the Dukes of Norfolk had for some time been trying to raise money to recoup their losses during the long period when their estates were forfeit to the Crown. Bradfer Lawrence records that at one time tenements were selling for anything up to ten times their normal price of from £20 to £30, which reflected the quite artificial demand created by valuable parliamentary votes.

We are fortunate in having a letter from the Rector of Castle Rising, the Rev Matthew Bolton, which he wrote to the lord of the manor in 1695 which tells the inside story of an election – not for parliament, but for the mayoralty of the Borough, and of the intrigue and trickery that were normally practised in those days. The story starts with the Walpoles making a determined effort to get their man nominated as Mayor. They must have felt that with the Rising Chase estate having just been purchased by a new Howard owner, that they must leave no stone unturned to break into the Howard stronghold, and that the best way of doing this was to nominate a mayor who could be expected to favour their cause. The rector, seeing what was going on, and being loyal to his patron who had appointed him to the living, decided to frustrate their plans.

The Walpole nomination for mayor was a man called Haten, and the plan was to prevent the rector nominating a rival candi-

* In 1695 the Walpoles had acquired some 25 of the 60 votes in Rising.

date, which only he had the power to do, by trumping up a charge against him, and calling in the bailiffs from Lynn to arrest not only him but also the serving mayor, so that both of them would be safely under lock and key on the day the nomination had to be made. Fortunately the rector got wind of the plan, and in the early morning of election day, he and the mayor went into the church and secured themselves within the tower of the church, where they got a good view of what was going on in the village. In concert with Mr Cussand, the lord's agent, they had previously managed to find a person who they persuaded to stand as mayor. The nomination ceremony was normally held in the church, so this seemed a good way of avoiding the bailiffs who were looking for him.

The rector recounts that he and the mayor had a fine prospect out of the steeple every way and saw the participants in the day's struggle arrive one by one, and also saw the bailiffs quartering the town looking for them. It puzzled me at first that he called the tower of the church a steeple, for I had thought that a steeple was the same thing as a spire, but when I looked it up, I found that a tower is, and always had been known as a steeple.

Things however did not work out quite as he expected, because the head of the Walpole family, Colonel Walpole, then arrived, and after learning that the rector had had to go into hiding, expressed his displeasure at the action of his supporters, and called off the bailiffs. Truth is indeed stranger than fiction, because at this moment a letter from Thomas Howard arrived for Colonel Walpole supporting his cause, so that the rector was able to emerge from his steeple, and all ended happily, with felicitations to the rector, and discomfiture of the bailiffs and their supporters.

The rector's account also told of the sumptuous fare provided at the Haten's house by the Walpoles, which included wine and old Hogen Venison Pasty, Roast Beef and many other good dishes, but did not say whether he patronised this feast or the one provided at the Mayor's house. On the whole, seeing that he must have known just what was laid on for dinner, I think he must have dined at Haten's. He also tells us that Haten 'did not recover from his dump all day', which is I suppose another way of saying that he was thoroughly fed up by finding out that his disloyalty to the Howard cause and his dirty tricks had recoiled against him.

The Mayor

Rising had a mayor from very early times, and the earliest known mayor was elected in 1275. His name – dating from before the time when surnames were regularly used – was Robert le Mayre. He was a man of some local importance because it was he, in consultation with the lord of the manor and his agent, who exercised the functions of policeman, jailer, food and market inspector and general settler of local disputes, quite apart from being the returning officer at parliamentary elections.

The mayor had a sargent to assist him in his duties, no doubt in apprehending wrongdoers and keeping them securely locked up in the dungeon of the Castle until it was convenient to send them to Swaffham Bridewell for custody, and to Norwich for trial and sentence. It would seem that the lord of the manor had the job of swearing the mayor into his office, and this duty was generally delegated to the agent. The declaration which had to be made at the swearing-in ceremony – almost certainly in the church – is a good example of the close relationship which existed between the church and the civil authority. It appears that the mayor could not possibly be a Catholic, because no one of that religion could possibly have signed such a declaration:

I Nathaniel Kirby Mayor of the Borough of Castle Rising
in the County of Norfolk Do Declare that I do believe that –
there is not any Transubstantiation in the Sacrament of the
Lords Supper or in the Elements of Bread and Wine at or after
the Consecration thereof by any Person whatsoever.
This Declaration was made & Subscribed
the thirty first Day of October 1765. — Nathaniel Kirby
before me
Richd Fawssett

Richard Fawssett was the lord of the manor's agent at the time.

A later Mayor, John Wakefield, is commemorated by a tombstone in the churchyard which records that he was 'Mayor of this Corporation twenty-seven times', and on the same stone – his wife

Mary Wakefield, who 'was Mayoress of this Corporation nineteen times'. He died some years after his wife aged ninety in 1796. It was not always easy to persuade somebody to stand for election as mayor, although he received a salary from the estate of £13-6-8d, as well as a field called The Mayor's Carr, the crops from which would no doubt have been his perquisite. A letter from Thomas Fawssett in 1791 reports

> 'I have just returned from a visit to Rising where I have been for the purpose of attending the choice of Maior for the ensuing year, My brother has again taken this office, but with some reluctance....'

In 1778 the Mayor of that time applied to the state for a gown to be supplied for his use and this had the personal attention of the Lord Suffolk, who was the Howard owner at that time, and his letter has survived

> Fawssett,
> This is the first time I have heard he wished to have one. I desire you to bespeak one – such a one as you say he had before, for it is not becoming that anyone else should give him one. The warp should be of sufficient thickness and the material good and strong.
>
> Suffolk.

The Public Houses

No chapter on the life of the village would be complete without some reference to the places in which at least some of the residents spent part of their leisure time. We know from the account of the disbursements made by the agent at election times, that there were six public houses which divided the sum of £12 between them in 1688. We have little idea of the sort of places they were, except that they would have been very small. The Black Horse in its original position on the north-west corner of the cross roads was probably the largest, then there was the White Hart near the present rectory, and the Blue or Blow or Blowy Parlor just to the south-east of the Market Green. The Swan seems to have been just to the north of the Hospital, but I do not know the site of the Bull – a ruinous burgage – existing in 1579. That makes five pubs, which still leaves one missing name. There would seem little doubt that the main reason for their existence was the liberal disbursements made at election times.

We can trace the position of most of them by studying their burgage agreements, and I quote a part of one of them to show how properties were located with reference to others.

> This Indenture made the ninth day of ffebruary in the 13th year of the reign of our Sovereign Lord George . . . by the Grace of God of Great Britain, ffrance, and Ireland king defender of the ffaith Anno Domii 1726 between Mary Robinson of North Wootton in the County of Norfolke Sprinster, only daughter and heiress of John Robinson late of North Wootton aforesaid Yeoman of the one parte and Roger Plattfoot of North Wootton Yeoman of the other parte . . . doth bargain and sell all that free Burgage and Tenement with the Barns Stables Outhouses Gardens and Orchards known by the name of the Blow Parlor together with half a rood of land . . . lying in Castle Riseing next a place there commonly called the Markett Green on the north part and the tenement and burgage late John Bennet on the south parte and abutting on the common highway leading from the Markett Green towards the Castle . . . to have and to hold etc . . .

At least one of the pubs brewed its own beer, for an agreement exists for the sale of the brewing fittings and fixtures of the Black Horse in 1850 – 'and also all the brewing Plant, Coppers and appurtenances attached thereto, also the barrels, casks and stock in trade connected with the public house and brewery . . .' There are occasional mentions of the pubs in letters from the agent, for example he says that in 1801 'the public houses are all let without lands at £20 per year . . . they would be let at much more to an indifferent tenant . . .' This rather odd statement I suppose means that 'an indifferent person' was someone unknown to him.

Another letter about the Black Horse in 1809 says: We have been under the necessity of changing the tenant of the Black Horse, his affairs got so embarrassed he could not continue. I secured the rent, and I have replaced Moyes with an exceptionally safe and I hope a useful tenant.' Perhaps he did well because a year or two later we read of stabling for four to six horses being provided at the same pub.

The Game

There is little reference to game in the correspondence, although there are occasional reports of the prosecution of poachers, but one gets the impression that not much was done to preserve the game until the early part of the nineteenth century. Two gamekeepers' cottages were built in the 1850's and perhaps it was the coming of the railways with easier and quicker transport of game to urban markets that made it imperative to have a better conservation policy. A most interesting letter from Lord Suffolk brings the Black Horse into our story again

> I received the enclosed letter this morning, I don't like these licentious proceedings and wish some method could be hit upon to prevent them. If partridges grow scarce you may discontinue sending them, but if you could send up a few pheasants now and then I should be glad. Somebody certainly must be procured to look after the game. The Keeper of a public house does not seem to me just the person to be trusted with it. The charge requires diligence and spirit, and like all others, honesty. If you think the man at the Black Horse has the quality, and may be trusted, his being a publican may be overlooked(, but I rather think it is a dangerous precedent.
> Duke Street I am, etc Suffolk
> Nov 27 1777

I don't know to what he is referring in his first sentence, but it looks to me rather like a reference to a Castle Rising Election. He clearly mistrusted publicans, and I imagine it was rather unlikely the tenant of the Black Horse got the job, as Suffolk's agent would hardly be likely to have pressed the case in the light of his master's opposition. Game was served on special occasions as we can see from the following letter of 26 October 1809:

> Sir, Your letter informing me of your being prevented from visiting Norfolk this season arrived in due course to the great disappointment of everyone here; Immediately on its receipt, I wrote the brewer at Setch (Mr Herbert) who had sent in five barrels of Ale and five of table beer, apprising him of your being

prevented from coming to Rising and requesting him to take them again, offering to make him such recompence as he might think reasonable. He very handsomely sent for the barrels in a few days, with a civil letter saying that as you had not had occasion for the beer he would readily take it again. All the other things that were provided here will be used without any loss or inconvenience.

Mr Holland will tomorrow be sworn into the office of Mayor, I directed John Brown to kill some Game for his Feast as usual; As Burgess Clarke who assisted John Brown during the last season in preserving the game, and seems to be very active and industrious, I thought it right to engage him during the present season from the end of his harvest till the first week in February at six shillings per week, he seems quite satisfied, and has promised to use his best exertions in the service.

This is the only mention I have seen that a Mayoral Feast was held each year, a custom which I think might well be re-instituted – for the benefit of course of the Chairman of the Parish Council, the Mayor's successor, and his six fellow burgesses. I do however declare an interest in this matter!

The Rector and the Church

We know that the village saw very little of the lord of the manor, just an occasional visit when he stayed either with the agent or at the Hall, and the agent himself rarely if ever lived in the village, as one can see from his correspondence, where one frequently meets such a comment as 'I have just come back from Rising where I went to swear in the Mayor' or 'it was terrible to see the storm damage when I visited Rising yesterday'. We saw that it was the Rector who told the lord of the manor about the happenings at the election in 1695, and over a hundred years later in a letter from the agent, James Bellamy, dated 26 October 1809 we hear news of the intention to build a new rectory:

I have received a letter from the Rev Mr Fawssett, of which I feel it is my duty to send you the following extracts: 'The intention of building a Residence at Castle Rising which I expressed to you is now fully determined, and I have much satisfaction in communicating that the plan, which has been submitted to Mr

> Howard, received his entire approbation, and he has given me full power to procure brick earth, or to raise Carr Stone for the purpose, and it is my intention to be getting as forward this winter as I can, that the work may be finished during the summer'. If you have any observation to favour me with on this subject they shall be duly attended to. I conclude you know that the bricks for your use have been made from the Common of Castle Rising, and the Carr Stone raised from out of the Lodge Farm.

Now this suggests that he may have lived elsewhere, possibly at Congham or at Roydon, both of which parishes were at one time or another associated with Rising. But the main thing the letter tells us is that the new Rectory succeeded the old Parsonage House in 1810. We know that the Parsonage was on the same spot as the present rectory from the estate map of 1732, on which it is marked and named. By inference it also tells us that the Parsonage must have been a rather inferior residence or at least that it was in a bad enough state of repair to require the building of a new house.

The status of the parson was much higher in the nineteenth century than in earlier times, and a two-hundred-year-old house in 1800 would be unlikely to have offered the kind of accomodation that would have been expected by an incumbent of a country parish at this time. The new rectory is well built and has spacious rooms, and its grounds of three acres have been enlarged to take in surrounding properties including those of the old White Hart which used to adjoin it.

It is difficult to overstress the importance of the church in the life of the village. When William d'Albini II destroyed the old church in building his castle, he lost no time in building the new one using the same high quality limestone he used for his castle, because this was the Norman way and this pattern was repeated all over the country. The inhabitants no doubt had to work very hard in building the new structures – just look at the huge task it must have been to erect those huge earthworks round the keep – and they were no doubt paid little enough for doing so, but their new masters believed passionately in the importance of looking after a man's soul, and it is to that belief that we owe our wonderful heritage of church buildings up and down the country.

The Normans and those who came after them saw to it that

as far as possible no one was further away from a church than he was from his work, and in this part of Norfolk few people had to walk more than two to three miles to attend their place of worship. One would like to know more than we do of the happenings in the life of the church and the parson, but what is of interest to us was of not sufficient interest for any of the incumbents to make a record of the events, with the one exception we have already reported. Nevertheless, there are quite a few things that give an insight into the part the church played in the village.

For instance it is recorded that on one occasion the church was used to claim the ancient privilege of sanctuary. This is what happened as recorded in the Coroners Rolls

> Be it remembered that on the Wednesday next after the feast of All Saints the 2nd year of the year of King Richard II [1378-9] in the church of Castel Rysyng John Baxter of Fullyng Newton before John Bacheler of Swaffam coroner of the Lord the King in the presence of John Boteler, Robert Mathew etc. acknowledged himself to be a felon of the Lord the King, because he was on the Monday in the Feast of All Saints about the hour of twilight at Babynglee killed Lawrence Costyn for which felony he fled to the aforesaid church. Being asked whether he wished to surrender himself to the peace of the Lord the King by the said coroner in the presence of the said jurors he altogether denied it, seeking that he might abjure the kingdom of England as a felon of the Lord the King, whereof an inquest having been taken there before the coroner by the said jurors – they say that John Baxter feloniously killed Lawrence Costyn. John abjured the Kingdom of England, and the port of Ipswich was given for crossing the sea within 14 days. The said felon had no goods.'

Such a privilege of sanctuary dated from the time when the church had its own laws, but I do not know what would have happened to the felon once he had landed in a foreign country.

We have seen how the influence of the church required that the Mayors of the Borough should sign a declaration that they did not believe in the Catholic doctrine of transubstantiation, and while these things may seem surprising to us, they were accepted as a normal part of village life, just as were other habits and customs imposed by the church. For example, some people may have wondered about the purpose of the little door high up to the north of the main arch between the Nave and the tower, and may not have realised that this door gave access to the rood loft which spanned the church above the Nave, and which had a crucifix, and that it was the habit at Easter to keep watch all night. The Puritan tide swept these away, and only the little door bears witness to the slow change in religious thought over the centuries.

The Victorians made many changes, and I fear they are much reviled today for the thoroughness with which they swept away the old box pews and other emblems of former ages. It must be remembered however that they were not the first generation to destroy so much that was beautiful in our churches, for the Puritans were far worse in smashing the painted glass (I purposely use the former term in use in Rising), and the lovely statuary and ornamentation which our ancestors found so much to their taste, and the fact that we have suffered at least two periods of vandalism in our history must point to some defect in the character of the race that allowed such things to happen. It is worth quoting what was said about the church by William Taylor in his book *The History and Antiquities of Castle Rising*

> 'The Nave is fitted up with goodly rows of open benches,– no closed pew here presents a heartless barrier to the penitent, who comes weary and heavy laden to seek him who has promised rest:– happily the day is not far distant when open seats will require a remark, closed pews are already felt to be a disgrace to a national church.'

The 'goodly rows of benches' are firmly fixed to the floor and the huge size and the weight of the stalls almost hidden behind the Nave arch effectively imposes Victorian ideas of church worship on us some 130 years after their installation. What a mercy it is that the orders of worship of the Anglican church were not changed by the Victorians, for heaven only knows what enormities they might have perpetrated. People sometimes complain of the archaic language of 1662, but at least it was beautiful, and when I listen to the glorious English of Matins and Evensong I often think of what someone once said to me about them '. . . its hymns and prayers are smooth with use; they hold a memory of past generations'.

Nevertheless the history of a church such as ours shows that considerable changes have occurred in both the fabric and the furnishings. The lancet windows in the Chancel are of Henry III's reign (1216-72) and replaced earlier Norman windows. Then we had the period of the rood loft which involved cutting the entrance door to the loft high up in the west wall of the tower.

Cotman's drawing of 1811 shows a chancel with a communion table hemmed in and almost hidden by a litter of old timber, curtains and hassocks that would be unthinkable in the chancel of today. In Victorian days an ornate gothic reredos was placed behind a new communion table demonstrating the new emphasis on this sacrament which is still very much with us. In the 1970's a vandal broke off all the little stone rosettes which decorated this reredos.

We would like to know much more than we do about the reason for the major reconstructions of Victorian days. Salvin was the architect for the 1845-49 rebuilding in which the tower was provided with a saddle roof, and one presumes that he copied the entrance building of the Castle Keep, which according to old illustrations always had one. It is difficult to see why Street, the architect of the reconstruction in the 1880's, thought it necessary to rebuild the south transept and add to the height of the tower so short a time after the 1849 rebuilding. Perhaps he thought the additions made the building more imposing. It is fortunate that plans for the erection of a northern transept at this time were not proceeded with.

In writing a history of the village, events which were worthy of being called 'news' were not very common. Nevertheless, I feel sure that the Rector of Rising had plenty to occupy his time, and he would have regarded it a very slack week if he had not to perform any marriages, baptisms and funerals in the course of the month. He nevertheless was occupied with the hundred and one things which used to go on in a church. There was the care of the bells, of which there were three originally, there is only one now, made in 1660 by Thomas Norris of Norwich. There were the reconstructions, alas not always very good ones, such as the removal of the Isabella slab in the old church porch which some people used to think was her tombstone, but which, of course, was nothing of the sort, because Isabella lay buried in the city church of Greyfriars Newgate in London. There was the installation of the painted glass west front window – there is a mystery about this, because Mr

Bellamy in a letter of 1812 to Richard Howard at Ashstead asks confirmation that he is to pay the Rev Richard Fawssett £60-12-6 for 'the purchase carriage and other expenses attending the placing of a figure of painted glass in the Western window – which he says you desired might be to your charge'. Now the present west window is one to Greville Howard presumably put there by Mary Howard as a memorial to her husband. Did she, one wonders, remove the 1812 window and perhaps send it to her other estate at Levens as she did one of the Rising bells in 1841?

There will always be mysteries of this kind, for the only records the church appears to have are the registers of births, marriages and burials which still moulder away in the church safe, and these we owe to Henry VIII's Chancellor Thomas Cromwell who decreed that every parish church should keep such records. I think we owe him a lot, because in England we have the finest records of this kind anywhere in the world. Our own register shows as the first entry

Castle Rysyng – Marriages
July 10th 1573 BARVELLES – Yonge William and Agnes

The first baptism recorded was Aug 20th 1573 – John Selbye, and the first burial somewhat later – Feb 28th 1605 – Mason.

We are fortunate in having a number of drawings of the church and the castle, probably the most famous of which are by John Sell Cotman who not only recorded scenes all over Norfolk but in 1811 and 1813 published etchings, no less than five of which were of Castle Rising church. One of them (used as an illustration of a leaflet on sale in the church) is of the triple lancet windows in the chancel.

So ends the story of Castle Rising, a story which of course is not at an end. We are now a 'conservation' village and we are now trying to look at our village, as it were, through a new pair of glasses. I told earlier that when William d'Albini II built his castle home here, the village was laid out in a carefully planned manner, with the church and the market green adjoining each other on the road from the castle to the harbour. They certainly left us a wonderful heritage which we are proud to share with the many visitors who come to see a wealth of buildings preserved so well over many centuries. I only hope that we shall do as well in the future as our ancestors did in the past.